teeth

by Susan Baker

illustrated by Joanna Stubbs

MACDONALD
3 4 5

I brush my teeth every morning
and every night.
I like squeezing out the toothpaste.

I rinse the brush
under the tap afterwards.
Then I put it back in the rack
next to Daddy's.

I look in the mirror to make sure that
there are no bits of food left
in the gaps between my teeth.
I feel my teeth with my tongue,
they feel all smooth and shiny.
There are ten at the bottom
and ten at the top.

My front teeth have sharp edges.
I use them to bite my food.
I like the pattern they make
when I bite a cheese sandwich.

My back teeth are big and knobbly.
I use them to chew my food.
If I have a biscuit to eat,
my back teeth can crunch it up quickly.

My baby sister has her food mashed up
because she can't chew very well.
She hasn't got her back teeth yet.
She has four front teeth.
When a new tooth
was coming through her gum
it made her cry.
Mummy gave her a teething ring to bite on.

My big cousin had a wobbly tooth.
It fell out in our kitchen
when we were eating apples.
Now he has a gap in his teeth.
His grown up teeth
will come through soon.

You get your grown up teeth
after you start school.
They are waiting in your gums
and when they are ready
they push the baby teeth out
one by one.
They have to last you forever,
until you are as old as granny.
So you should look after them carefully
and eat food that is good for them.

The dentist told me that carrots
and celery are the best snacks
to nibble between meals.
You shouldn't eat too many
sweet sugary things because
sugar makes holes in your teeth.

I go to the dentist twice a year
to make sure my teeth are all right.
I like having a ride in the moving chair.
The dentist looks into my mouth
with a little mirror
and sometimes she touches my teeth
with a pointed tool.

When I say goodbye she always says,
'Come and see me again soon.
Remember to brush your teeth every day
and don't eat sweets between meals !'

Notes

Learning about teeth is one of the most useful discoveries that children can make about their bodies. There are dramatic developments to watch, from the eruption of a baby's first tooth, to the last wiggle of a wobbly tooth as a 'grown up' second tooth starts to push its way through.

Babies can have a toothbrush as soon as the first tooth appears but don't let them crawl or run about with a toothbrush in their mouths.

Encourage your children to brush their teeth properly at least twice a day. Buy toothpaste with fluoride in it as this helps to strengthen the teeth. Find out if the water in your home has fluoride in it. If not you can give your child fluoride drops or tablets. Your dentist will be able to advise you.

Sweet and sugary foods are bad for teeth but most children love them, so try to give them only at mealtimes, not between meals. The danger is not how much sugar you eat but how often. 'Making them last', is the worst way to eat sweets as it keeps the teeth coated in sugar all the time. A film of plaque forms on the teeth continuously. The sugar combines with this to make an acid which slowly eats away the protective enamel on the teeth. Once hardened, plaque is difficult to brush off. You can buy a disclosing agent from the chemist. This is fun to use occasionally and it helps you to see any remaining plaque by staining it bright pink.

Savoury snacks between meals are the safest and don't forget that too many sweet drinks can cause damage too. A drink of water after meals will at least rinse your mouth if brushing isn't possible.

Take your child for a dental check twice a year from the age of three even if nothing seems to be amiss. Visiting the dentist can be fascinating for children and if they eventually need treatment, they should have no fear.

© Macdonald & Co (Publishers) Ltd 1983

First published 1983 by
Macdonald & Co (Publishers) Ltd
Maxwell House
Worship Street
London EC2A 2EN

ISBN 0 356 07832 9

Consultants: Dr Iona Heath
Michele Ehrenmark
Editor: Lucille Powney
Art agency: B. L. Kearley Ltd
Production: Rosemary Bishop

Printed and bound by Purnell & Sons (Book Production) Ltd England